Hello. My name is Georgia, and I am 7

Guess what? I found the coolest stories about seven superwomen who did amazing stuff a long time ago.

It's like time-traveling but in a book!

So, let's go on this big adventure together and learn about these incredible women who made sure we can all have a say in things today.

Get ready for a wild ride filled with marches, speeches, and tons of girl power.

Are you excited? I am!

Let's jump into
the fun and discover
how these
cool heroines
changed the world!

In this book, I will be telling you about women who stood up for other women. They were all part of the "suffrage movement."

The suffrage movement was a big effort by people, especially women, who wanted to change the rules so that everyone, no matter their gender, could vote in elections.

In the past, only some people, mostly men, were allowed to vote, and women couldn't. The suffrage movement was about making things fair and letting women have the same right to vote as men. It took a lot of hard work, protests, and speaking out, but in the end, they succeeded, and today, everyone can vote to help agree on important decisions.

I will be sharing the stories of some women who changed the world!

Are you ready?

Sojourner Truth was born in New York in 1797. She was born into slavery because of her skin color. Even her name was given to her by her owner. She believed everyone should be free and tried to make that happen.

In 1826, Sojourner escaped! She did not stop there. She thought her mission was to help other people find their...FREEDOM! So she did.

In 1851, Sojourner Truth made a speech called "Ain't I A Woman?". In her speech, she asked why women aren't treated equally to men and reminded everyone that they deserve respect and freedom, too.

Freedom and equality were connected in people's minds because of her.

Even though she faced many challenges as a person of color, she continued to fight for equality and freedom. She definitely had a growth mindset!

Her work changed the world, and her speeches inspired people to stand up for what was right. One person's voice can make a big difference.

DID YOU KNOW?

A long time ago, brave women started asking for something very important - the right to vote! This big effort to make sure everyone, including women, could have a say in important decisions lasted for many years.

Harriet Taylor Upton

Harriet Taylor Upton was born in Ohio, USA, on December 17, 1853. She grew up in a time when women did not have many rights, but Harriet believed that women should have a say in the decisions that affected their lives. In other words, she believed that women should be able to vote.

Harriet went to school and was educated by smart teachers, and she learned about equality and justice. This inspired her to take action for women.

She became a leader in the suffrage movement and inspired many other women to stand up for their right to vote and encourage people to join the suffrage movement.

Harriet believed women should have the right to vote and say no to the laws they didn't like. She also believed that women should have the same rights as men.

She faced many challenges, but she never gave up. She even encouraged many other people to stand up for women.

Harriet Taylor Upton will be remembered as one of the women who fought for women's rights. We can remember her as an inspiration to stand up for what is right and make the world equal for both women and men.

DID YOU KNOW?

In 1848, something super cool happened in New York! A bunch of amazing people got together for the Seneca Falls Convention. It was likc the first-ever party where they talked about how girls and boys should have equal rights!

Alice Paul

Alice Paul was a creative and fearless woman who joined the suffrage movement.

She was born on January 11, 1885, in New Jersey. Her only thoughts were that women should have the same rights as men and wanted women to have the right to vote.

Alice went to college and learned about the suffrage movement. She was inspired by what she learned and decided to join the fight.

She organized parades and protests outside the White House and was even arrested! But that didn't stop her. She kept on going.

Because of Alice Paul and the other women we talk about in this book, women can now vote in elections. Back then, women were not even allowed to be part of elections. We can have a say in important decisions thanks to her and all the other people who supported her.

DID YOU KNOW?

Have you ever seen people wearing all white during celebrations? Well, during their big marches and rallies, these superhero ladies wore white to show everyone that they were pure and strong in their fight for girls' rights.

Lucy Burns

Lucy Burns was born in New York on July 28, 1879. She grew up in a time when women had fewer rights than men. But Lucy believed in fairness and that women should have the right to vote.

Lucy was a bright and determined woman. She had the opportunity to go to college and learn about the suffrage movement.

Lucy Burns was determined and not afraid to take bold actions to support the suffrage movement. She joined forces with Alice Paul to organize parades and pickets.

They were known as the "Silent Guards," who stood outside the White House silently holding signs demanding the right to vote for women.

Lucy and the other women in the suffrage movement faced many challenges and were horribly treated. But they were determined to make their voices heard and fight for equality.

Lucy Burns' hard work paid off when, in 1920, women were allowed to vote! Her dedication and bravery were important in making this happen.

Lucy Burns taught us to stay strong and keep going no matter what we face. She showed that by staying strong and determined, change is possible.

Today, women have the right to vote thanks to the dedication of suffragists like Lucy Burns. Her story reminds us that we should never be afraid to fight for our beliefs and that our voices can make a real difference in the world.

DID YOU KNOW?

Imagine two superhero friends named Susan B. Anthony and Elizabeth Cady Stanton. They weren't fighting bad guys, but they were on a mission to make sure girls had the same chances as boys. They were like real-life superheroes for girls everywhere!

Susan Anthony

Susan also grew up when women did not have as many rights as men. They couldn't go to work or school like we do or even vote in elections. But Susan knew this wasn't fair, and she decided to do something about it.

Susan was born on February 15, 1820, in Massachusetts. As Susan grew up, she joined the fight for women's rights. She traveled all over the country, giving speeches and sharing her beliefs. She believed that if women had the right to vote, they could help make important decisions to make the world a better place for everyone.

In 1848, Susan and her friend Elizabeth Cady Stanton organized a special meeting. They wrote a powerful document. This announcement said that women should have the same rights as men, including the right to vote.

Susan got in trouble for speaking out. But she never gave up. She said, "Failure is impossible." She knew the fight for women's rights was too important to stop.

In 1920, women won the right to vote thanks to her and many other brave women. Susan's dream finally came true!

DID YOU KNOW?

Picture this: girls and women having a big gathering in the streets! They marched together, held up colorful signs, and even had awesome floats. It was like a parade to tell everyone how much they wanted girls to have the right to vote.

Elizabeth Cady Stanton

Elizabeth was born on November 12, 1815, in New York. She grew up in a time when women had very few rights. They couldn't own a house, couldn't go to college, and they couldn't even vote in elections.

Elizabeth came from a big family, and her dad was a lawyer. He wasn't like other dads who were telling their daughters everything they couldn't do, but instead, he encouraged her to think for herself and be independent. These values shaped her belief in women's rights.

When Elizabeth became a grown-up, she and her friend Susan B. Anthony organized an important meeting. At this meeting, they wrote a powerful document about how women should have rights and that women should vote!

Elizabeth traveled, gave speeches, and wrote about women's rights. She believed that if women had the right to vote, they could improve the world. She knew it would be a tough battle, but she was determined to make a difference.

Elizabeth faced many rough and tough challenges along the way. People told her that women shouldn't be involved in making decisions, but she didn't listen. She fought with all her heart.

Elizabeth Cady Stanton's hard work paid off. She didn't live to see women win the right to vote, but in 1920, women won the right to vote in the United States. Elizabeth's dream came true because of her dedication and the dedication of many other brave women.

DID YOU KNOW?

You know what's super cool? Even kids like you were part of this big adventure! Boys and girls, just like you, joined in and became "suffragettes." They believed that everyone, no matter their age, should have a fair chance in making the world a better place.

Ida B. Wells

In a time when justice was not always served, a courageous woman named Ida B. Wells fearlessly fought for equality and justice for all.

Ida B. Wells was born on July 16, 1862, in Mississippi. She grew up in a world where there was slavery against people of color. Despite all the challenges she faced, Ida believed in equal rights and worked tirelessly to make the world a fairer place.

Ida was a strong-minded and intelligent young woman. She became a teacher and a journalist, using her words to expose the injustices she saw. She knew it was her duty to stand up for what was right.

One of Ida's most important missions was to raise awareness about lynching, a terrible act of violence and hatred against African Americans. She wrote articles and gave speeches to shine a light on this issue and demand change.

Ida fought not only for African Americans' rights but also for women's rights. She believed that everyone should have a voice in the decisions that affected their lives.

Today, we remember Ida B. Wells as a champion for equality and justice. Her story inspires us to speak out against unfairness, stand up for all people's rights, and work towards a world where everyone is treated with justice and respect.

DID YOU KNOW?

Guess what happened in 1920? A special rule called the 19th Amendment was created! It was like a magic spell that said, "Hey everyone, girls can vote too!" This made sure girls' voices were heard when important decisions were made.

In the end, the stories of these brave women who stood up for what they believed in teach us an important lesson: that even the smallest voices can join together to make a big, powerful voice.

Though some of these amazing women didn't live long enough to see the day when all women could vote in 1920, their courage and determination paved the way for a brighter future.

Now, we can all celebrate the fact that every girl and every boy, just like you and me, has the right to have their voice heard.

So, let's remember these heroes and their incredible journey, and always stand up for what we believe is right!

Made in the USA
Monee, IL
06 February 2024